COURTROOM CONFESSIONS

WHEN THE SPECIAL INDEPENDENT PROSECUTOR'S OFFICE WAS ACQUITTED AT THE FEDERAL COURT

JOSÉ ENRICO VALENZUELA ALVARADO

CREDITS

Author: José Enrico Valenzuela Alvarado
www.valenzuelalaw.net
https://www.facebook.com/joseenricova
jeva@valenzuelalaw.net

Editor: Yasmín Rodríguez for The Writing Ghost®
Translation & production: The Writing Ghost®
www.thewritingghost.com

Cover art: Gil Acosta
www.gilacosta.com
Portrait of the author by: Alex Rafael Román
alexrafaelroman@yahoo.com

Library of Congress Control Number 2019902423

ISBN 978-1-7337271-1-2

First Edition, 2021

TESTIMONIALS

"In times like these when the Special Independent Prosecutor's Office (SIP) is under fire and lost the people's trust, the book *Courtroom Confessions* by José Enrico Valenzuela Alvarado, Esq. provides a solid reference point for rewriting a new mission and vision statement for this public resource to effectively fight corruption; above all, total independence. Two decades have passed. Several of the individuals mentioned in this book are still active in partisan politics, and they should be held responsible for their actions by the public. There is much to do, much to teach, but first, there needs to be a genuine commitment from elected officials and those nominated to serve to not take advantage of their situation at the public's expense."

Manuel Ernesto Rivera
Independent Journalist

"The book *Courtroom Confessions* captivated me from beginning to end. It's an easy read, but extremely interesting. The author captures the reader's attention by clearly and concisely exposing one of the highest-profile cases in our island's legal and political history."

Luis Enrique Falú
Journalist

"Valenzuela Alvarado Esq. keeps the readers' interest by navigating between personal and professional retrospection in a way that gives a unique sense of relevance to the text. This is a very interesting book about one of the topics that generated the most debate in the legislature: the efficiency of the SIP and the cronyism in Puerto Rico's politics in a solid court case full of partisan nuances."

Dr. Jorge Suárez Cáceres
Doctor of Criminal Justice

"*Courtroom Confessions* is a clear example of the sacrifices that go with a career in the legal system. Those who have just passed the bar and have an illusion of justice will receive 'shock therapy' when entering the practice, especially in the public sector. Nevertheless, it's a vital part of Valenzuela Alvarado, Esq.'s motivation to be victorious for his clients."

Fabiana Piñeda Naredo
Third year Law Student

"My colleague, José Enrico Valenzuela, honestly and transparently tells a tale of his trajectory through the Department of Justice and the impact caused by his participation in a case plagued by the political tribalism in our country. The story's clarity and honesty allow the author to free the skeletons in the closet that have weighed on his soul. At the same time, the reader can understand the adventures, complications and consequences of litigation and how much a legal professional can put on the line to remain brave and honorable. The author was able to do more than just a courtroom confession: he bared his soul."

Sharon M. Hernández López, Esq.

"Putting the country ahead of the individual is perhaps the most critical lesson in José Enrico's experiences. Here, he tells of his time defending the people's representatives so that they could retain their immunity while investigating and prosecuting those we trust to administrate our country, Puerto Rico. It is important to learn the history of those who have walked through the agonizing trial by fire that is 'politics' in Puerto Rico. Many of us have had to reinvent ourselves thanks to the political influence that pervades far too many public and private workplaces."

Juan C Sellas Hernández, J.D.

"Valenzuela Alvarado Esq. achieved a detailed narrative with all the missing information about the federal case Jorge Aponte Hernández v. the SIP. The book masterfully describes the external aspects of the case that affected the process of preparing the pleadings and the opinions of the protagonists. It's required reading for all legal professionals in P.R."

Ramón A. Torres Cruz, Esq.

"*Courtroom Confessions* allows you to learn how the Department of Justice, the Office of the Special Independent Prosecutor, and Puerto Rico courts operate. It also demonstrates how lawyers live day-to-day while fighting for justice and truth to prevail when what is presented and said in court isn't what happened. The author captivates the reader with his personal life drama while struggling with the most important case of his career. You can see how both things intertwine and how he maintains his personal and professional values against all adversity and shows us how, even when everything is against you, in the end truth and perseverance always triumphs. This book lets you in on the details of criminal justice professions, where opportunists abound and few are loyal, and where you can only count on your intelligence and ethical values."

Fernando Fernández
International Private Investigator

"With a candid and enjoyable style, Valenzuela Alvarado, Esq. makes us participants on the other side of the coin in a notorious legal case. *Courtroom Confessions* shows us the metamorphosis and the human struggle that lawyers that prefer to defend just causes go through. In this case, an unjustified attack against the government's investigative branch and how the partisan political machine influences the crucible of justice. This is a book not only for those disillusioned with the legal practice but also for new lawyers that are interested in pursuing justice."

Fernando J. Nieves Camacho, Esq.

DEDICATION

To my parents, Patricia and José, thank you for conspiring with a higher power to bring me into this world, to Puerto Rico.

TABLE OF CONTENTS

ACKNOWLEDGEMENTS

To those who believe in me, and those who are no longer on this terrestrial plane but still care for me and protect me. You know who you are.

JUSTICE ABOVE ALL

It was November of 2006 in Puerto Rico. Thanksgiving had come and gone and Christmas was already in the air. Temperatures were beginning to drop and you could smell that strange scent of the holidays that nobody can quite explain, but everyone recognizes. The extremists were already searching for the perfect tree to decorate and ready for *parrandas*, our version of caroling, which involves lively music, dancing, and booze. People in the office were practicing for the upcoming parties and, especially on Fridays, the focus was on planning the fun for the weekend.

That Friday, I had finished my work for the day. It was 6:30 p.m. and I was ready to go pick up the lady who was my wife back then to go out to a few social gatherings. One of these "gatherings" was a party where the friend who invited us had pulled out all the stops and promised the best wine, beer, and appetizers. It goes without saying that I was dying to get out of the office.

I'm a very responsible person and very careful with my work, but I love to go out and have fun. Those who know me know that I'm not shy, but I am not the life of the party either. I enjoy family gatherings most of all and try to travel and explore both on my island and abroad. But, I also enjoy these social outings that characterize us Puerto Ricans, where you can always find the best food and music and it's quite easy to have a good time. At the time of this story, it was important to share these moments of fun and leisure with my wife. We had very little time together, every moment was precious, and the opportunity to spend time out as a couple was necessary and welcomed.

Just so I didn't feel guilty, and because of my habit of putting work first, I decided to check my internal mail before leaving. There, I found a new case assigned to me with the instruction that I see to it personally and to handle it ASAP. The case was that of Jorge Aponte Hernández, ex-director of Puerto Rico's Office of Management and Budget, who decided to counter-sue the former members of the Special Independent Prosecutor's Office (SIP) that brought a misappropriation of public funds case against him during a real estate acquisition. In his lawsuit, Jorge Aponte Hernández alleged, among other things, political persecution.

I already knew about the case because the accusation of malfeasance had been ongoing for several years. The judge's decision to dismiss the charges was viewed as controversial by the media and the legal community. Of course, what was supposed to be a quick peek at the file turned into a full reading that had me in the office until midnight and ruined all the party plans.

This was a very serious case. Hard evidence justified the original accusations of misappropriation of funds. My peers had done their job, but the judge dismissed the case *De motu proprio* as they say in Latin or, in more colloquial terms, "Because he felt like it," and the case was closed. The accused felt he had a right to protest his unjust accusation without any real evidence to prove there was any injustice.

There began a litany of war inside my head. The prosecutors had done their due diligence, investigated, gathered evidence, and brought the case to court. How could it be that he is now accusing them personally in a federal district court in Puerto Rico for doing their job? What about the immunity provided to protect prosecutors that represent the state?

The plaintiff based his lawsuit on a judge's decision. I mean, it's not like it was a frivolous case; rather, it was based on sound legal reasoning. I couldn't understand how the case existed in the first place, but I did understand that answers wouldn't come quickly and that my colleagues' future, as well as the respect for prosecutors everywhere, were in my hands.

When I decided to open that case file to take a quick look, I changed my life in many ways. It was the beginning of a great many things to come and the end to others. But, looking back, I can see that the decision I made that day was the correct one.

I decided to swim against the current, risk my future in the public service, create enemies, and change my family life altogether. On the other hand, I also decided that justice comes first; external influences are no match for intelligence and observation; and that when you have the truth on your side, winning is the only option.

CHAPTER I

2006:

The accused accuses his accusers

In 2006, I was named Director of Legal Affairs of the Litigation Office of the Department of Justice, where I had worked since 2003. I landed the job immediately after I passed my bar exam. So, when I arrived in 2003, I came with all the expectations of doing justice and the romanticism of being a member of the noblest profession. In other words, I came with all the *naiveté* of a freshly graduated student.

By 2006, I had it quite clear that everything wasn't all rosy in the legal system and had already developed the necessary experience to understand that cynicism is an inherent quality in all lawyers. At this time, I had a reputation for being meticulous, responsible, and dedicated. Also, I was quite impulsive and didn't second-guess my decisions if I had decided something was worthwhile.

I established myself as a serious lawyer during my career, one that only presented solid arguments supported by hard evidence and facts. In my profession, I am known as a bit of a risky player. People know I am pretty thorough in my cases and able to present a complete accusation or defense without any holes to exploit. In reality, I'm always a bit more ballsy than careful. The secret is to consolidate all the information, find the result that I'm looking for, and make a very complete and detailed case from there. I always follow my instincts first.

My relationship with my coworkers at that point was polite and professional. We all got along well, and there was an environment of mutual respect. Even though I never made any close friends, I considered my colleagues to be good acquaintances who I actively enjoyed working with. Even today, if I run into one of them, they usually greet me with an exuberant, "Enrico!" or, if we were a little closer than that, "Rico!" (my long-time nickname).

I've never turned down a handshake or hug from my colleagues or coworkers, and that includes those that did not keep in touch with me after the events in this book. In my opinion, they have a problem, not me. If anyone has questions about my actions and they ask me directly, I have no problem answering them. Well, reasonable questions anyway. Nevertheless, I don't have to explain my actions or decisions to anyone, nor will I get caught up in rumors or hearsay. Because of all this, I think that if someone greets me amicably and I respond in kind, we'll both have a much better day.

The work environment was what pretty much everyone would consider "normal." Nine to six with an hour for lunch, and most of the workday was spent alone at a desk. We all had things going on in our private lives, but the instances when personal matters affected our work were few and far between.

Sometimes, the longest discussion we would have about a case happened while we waited for the elevator, or perhaps during a coffee break, or maybe even having lunch together if we were working on the same case. We all tried our best to stay late at the office to avoid the rush-hour traffic. However, this routine was disrupted whenever there was a complicated case. When that happened, it was lunch over the keyboard and being on phone calls or at appointments and meetings all day. Then, at the end of the day, packing up everything and taking your work home to get up extra early to keep working before having to go in for the next full day.

In my case, this change in routine happened quite often. I am very passionate about what I do. I don't like losing or coming up even either. There were many sleepless nights trying to tie up loose ends building cases that merited the time and attention. Not only did I spend quite a lot of my free time working, but when I was engrossed in a case, I didn't take breaks during the day either. I didn't have time for personal calls or to send messages that weren't related to the work at hand.

My social life was usually nonexistent, and I never gave it a second thought. When I am in the zone, I don't need to see anyone or talk to anyone. This brought me great professional satisfaction but wasn't great for my personal life or my marriage. It's not that I think this level of dedication, necessarily, would cause problems in a relationship, but in my case and my wife's case, it did.

In 2006, I was married to "María Irma" for three years. My home life was relatively peaceful. In the beginning, it seemed like we shared the same goals: progress at work; to develop our careers; obtain financial security; provide the resources necessary for a comfortable and practical life; and enjoy the things in life you learn to appreciate with maturity, like friends, family, vacations, etc. Until then, it seemed like the motivation behind our decisions was to not "rock the boat."

We tried to maintain this tranquility because our relationship didn't need much to start rocking the metaphorical boat. It had been at the point of capsizing for quite a while and sailing some pretty cold and inhospitable waters.

My parents raised me in the traditional way and with a lot of love. I always felt safe with them and in their dedication to me. I was able to grow up following my dreams and discovering new things without worry. On the other hand, my former wife was raised in a fragile and dysfunctional environment. Her basic needs weren't always met growing up, and she had to face difficult situations at quite a young age.

She needed to feel safe, and a lot of the security she felt came from having money available and never having to worry about the basics. In my case, my professional motivation didn't necessarily come from the amount of my paycheck but rather what I could achieve through my work. Knowing that what I was doing was helping in some small way to change the world for the better was my security. It goes without saying that these opposing world views caused some friction in our marriage.

The moment I received the assignment of the case of Jorge Aponte Hernández, the boat that was my marriage was sailing on some rough and turbulent seas. At some level, I knew that if I got involved with the case, it would change my relationship with my wife forever. Either way, at that moment, it was in my nature to dedicate my mind, body, and soul completely to defend the SIP and everything the office represented in our legal system. Even with my cynicism and experience working with the government, I still faithfully believed in justice and the systems designed to protect it.

On the other hand, subconsciously, I think I was looking for a reason to confront the reality of my marriage. It was time to face the changes that were coming either way, sooner or later. For these reasons, my assignment to the case was an opportunity to spread my wings on a professional and personal level.

When those documents made their way into my hands that Friday afternoon in November, they came with special instructions from the Auxiliary Legal Secretary. She wanted me to see to the case personally and urgently. The boss didn't make requests like this without a good reason. Our office ran pretty well—in an organized fashion within the chaos implied when you work for the government. To see a note assigning the case to me on an emergency basis piqued my curiosity.

When I hurriedly read the documents on my desk, I realized this was the lawsuit that Jorge Aponte Hernández was bringing against the ex-members of the SIP who had brought a case against him. The previous case, the reason for the lawsuit, was very well known in the legal community. It was heavily discussed in hallways, elevators, bathrooms, at the water cooler, and during luncheons.

Back then, I was very interested in the case. I remember doing research and reading quite a bit about the proceedings. I had many questions about the original case and why the judge dismissed it without reaching a trial by jury. Now, I had the second act in my hands; the accused now accuses his accusers.

The information I had up to this point came from what was available as public knowledge. The SIP or the Office of the Special Independent Prosecutor had accused Jorge Aponte Hernández of misappropriation of public funds. Meanwhile, the then Executive Director of Administration and Finance authorized the purchase of a building for an amount that was over 300% of the appraised price. The case was taken to court, presented by the independent prosecutors assigned to the SIP: Ana P. Cruz Vélez, Héctor M. Montañez Reyes y José Pérez Rodríguez.

As far as I understood, the case was presented correctly, with all the necessary evidence. It was a solid case for what was considered malfeasance of public funds. However, in a surprising and, in my opinion, suspicious move, the judge assigned to the case, the Honorable Bárbara SanFiorenzo, decided to dismiss the case in a peremptory way so that a jury never saw the case.

Thinking about all this information, I had no other choice but to leave the office for home just as the sun was rising. I knew I would have to face my wife's anger after going back on my promise to take her to a spectacular party. But I dismissed the thought. I didn't care about having another fight. I hadn't given much thought to the changes that accepting the case would imply in my life. My whole focus was on the details. I tried to remember as many of them as possible as I drove down those empty early morning streets.

Still thinking about the case, I didn't even worry about waiting at all the red lights (something that, at that hour of the morning, might be bad for your health in our little island of enchantment). At last, by the time I arrived at my apartment and finally parked, I realized that to understand the motivation behind this case, I needed to brush up on the details of what happened in 1999, when Jorge Aponte Hernández allegedly decided to use public funds for himself.

There began the investigation process of searching for all the angles of a story with many characters and more twists and turns than the ones the mountain roads of my island are famous for. That was my social life done and dusted because it would take long hours glued to my computer monitor to unravel the twisted tale that culminated in SanFiorenzo's decision.

1999 - 2005:

The People vs. Jorge Aponte Hernández

Jorge Aponte Hernández came from a very politically active family, firmly rooted in the New Progressive Party (PNP, as it's abbreviated in Spanish). His brother, Néstor Aponte Hernández, was the Representative for District #33. His other brother, José Aponte Hernández, was the Secretary-General for the New Progressive Party while Jorge was in his post at the Office of Administration and Finance. Actually, between 1999 and 2000, Néstor resigned from his position as Representative to become a Judge in the Puerto Rican Court of Appeals. It was José who replaced him in the House of Representatives. Jorge Aponte Hernández was the Director of the Office of Administration and Finance under Governor Pedro Roselló from 1997 until May 1999.

As per the *"Ley Orgánica de Gerencia y Presupuesto"* (Management and Budget Organic Law) legislation passed in 1980, the Office of Administration and Finance (OGP, as it's abbreviated in Spanish) had a primary purpose–helping the governor create a budget for the country. This meant advising the governor and the legislative assembly in affairs related to expenses, the planning and allocation of public funds, and the administration of the aforementioned. In other words, Aponte Hernández directed the agency that determined how government money could be used.

Since 1997, the OGP had a budget for the procurement of buildings for government offices and agencies. The buildings acquired could be either private or public. The resolution that gave access to these funds authorized the OGP to expropriate private buildings if deemed necessary. When the Department of Natural and Environmental Resources determined they needed to establish a branch in 1999, assigning those funds belonged to the OGP.

The OGP decided that the best option for the branch's location would be in a building on Barbosa Avenue that belonged to the private citizen Miguel Cabral Veras. This property cost him $1,900,000.00 a little more than a year before. In an incomprehensible act, the OGP didn't buy the building, nor did they enter into a process of expropriation to secure it. Instead, they entered into a negotiation where they would rent the property for eight months for a total cost of $630,000.00.

The building remained vacant during this time. Then started a series of appraisals based on the potential income the property could generate to inflate its price artificially. The OGP ended up purchasing the building for

$8,700,000.00, almost seven million dollars over what Cabral Veras bought it for a year earlier. If you add the amount that it cost to rent the building, the total cost to the OGP was nine million three hundred and thirty thousand dollars ($9,330,000.00).

> The obvious question is: Who stood to gain by inflating the cost of the property by more than 300 percent?

What could have gone unnoticed was thoroughly investigated. The Independent Commission to Investigate Government Transactions, better known as the Blue Ribbon Committee, named by then governor Sila M. Calderón, determined sufficient cause to investigate the transaction in 1999. On the 29th of November, 2002, the Office of the Oversight Board for the Special Independent Prosecutor presented a claim against Jorge Aponte Hernández, accusing him of malfeasance of public funds. This claim set in motion a series of trials in the judicial community that took three years to resolve.

At that time, the Office of the Oversight Board for the Special Independent Prosecutor, or SIP, was an autonomous administrative entity, both functionally and financially, from the executive branch. The office was composed of three actual members and two alternate members selected from former judges of the courts. The Office of the Oversight Board for the SIP is the mechanism in charge of conducting the investigations for any misconduct by the upper members of the government.

For a case to arrive at the Office of the Oversight Board for the SIP, the secretary of justice would have to complete a preliminary investigation and determine that there was sufficient cause to think that a criminal act or misdemeanor affected civil rights, public duty, or public funds. If this is true, the secretary will submit a report with a recommendation to name a Special Independent Prosecutor. The board then determines if they will name an SIP to lead the case.

So, for a case to have an SIP assigned, it would have to pass through two separate scrutiny processes: the Department of Justice and the Oversight Board for the SIP. The appointed Special Independent Prosecutor has investigative powers and procedural powers bestowed that guarantee an impartial and objective investigation of the possible criminal acts done by a public official.

I'm explaining it all to make it crystal clear that the cases that the SIP works on are not trivial or superfluous. When an SIP is assigned, it has already been concluded that there is sufficient evidence to continue investigating and presenting the case. The case of Jorge Aponte Hernández was no exception. Both the Department of Justice and the Oversight Board for the SIP had determined that something improper had happened during the property acquisition on Barbosa Avenue.

It's important to note how solid the proof presented by the SIP was at the time so that you can draw your conclusions about the outcome of the case that was brought to the court by the lawyers contracted by the SIP: Ana P. Cruz Vélez, Héctor M. Montañez Reyes, and José Pérez Rodríguez. This was the legal team that I represented afterward when Jorge Aponte Hernández sued them.

The assignation of funds for new building acquisitions in 1997 was done under a joint resolution, specifically resolution number 552. From now on, I'll refer to this resolution as R.C. 552. This resolution was significant in this case. From its language, you can tell that the temptation to commit crimes is more notorious than notable. For the uninitiated, a joint resolution is the same as a law. The difference is that while laws are permanent, resolutions are transitory and have a specific purpose. Once that purpose is fulfilled, they lose their validity. They have the same power as a law for all intents and purposes and carry the same legal obligations.

R.C. 552 assigned to the OGP (or rather, made them custodians of) the amount of eighty-one million one hundred and ten thousand dollars ($81,110,000.00) to acquire buildings, either publicly or privately owned. R.C. 552 also stipulates the mechanisms that the director of the OGP must use to acquire the buildings. In section three of R.C. 552, it states:

"When the properties are not governmental, the Director of the Office of Administration and Finance has the authority to initiate a process of expropriation and to take any measures necessary to comply with the purpose of this Joint Resolution."

At the beginning of 1998, the then Secretary of the Department of Environmental and Natural Resources (DRNA, as it's abbreviated in Spanish), Daniel Pagán Rosa, informed Jorge Aponte Hernández as director of the OGP that DRNA needed a building to change the location of its central offices and the rest of its department. This same Secretary Pagán Rosa was the one who identified the building at 306 Avenida Barbosa in Hato Rey as the best option for the new location.

Aponte Hernández sent a letter to the owner of the building, Sr. Miguel Cabral Veras, who was the president of American Parking System, Inc. In the letter, Aponte Hernández communicated to Cabral that he wished to negotiate a contract to purchase the building. The building was in disrepair; the OGP knew about this. Nevertheless, instead of negotiating a purchase, or starting a process of expropriation, what was negotiated with Aponte Hernández's full knowledge was a rental agreement for six months with a monthly rental fee of $60,000.00.

Supposedly, the OGP created this rental arrangement to renovate the building and have it in good condition for the DRNA to take possession once the sale was finalized. The reality was that the DRNA never moved into the building during this time, and no renovations ever took place. Even though the DRNA paid the rent, the money came from the funds assigned by R.C. 552, of which the OGP was the custodian. I want to make clear that in no part did R.C. 552 stipulate any provisions for renting properties.

Once the OGP finished the process of negotiating the sales contract, they completed the purchase of the building at a much higher cost than was first contemplated, seeing as that Cabral had bought the building only a year earlier for much less. These are the numbers that I was referring to earlier. The building at Barbosa 306 cost the OGP 300 percent more than Cabral had paid for it. Expropriation was never considered as a possibility during the negotiation process.

So, we're back to the initial question: Who stood to gain in this transaction? If we go by the tenet of investigators to follow the money, where did this extra 300 percent go? Whose pockets did it end up in?

On top of everything, there are witnesses. One of them was an operations director at the OGP when everything took place, Juan Emmanuelli.

– Prosecutor: So I ask you, Did Mr. Aponte have knowledge of this rental contract?

– Emmanuelli: Yes.

– Prosecutor: The meetings that were held with Mr. Miguel Cabral to discuss the proceedings for the rental contract with an option for purchase, did Aponte have knowledge of those?

– Emmanuelli: What the meeting was about? Yes.

– Prosecutor: How did you know that he was aware?

– Emmanuelli: Because I never attended a meeting like that without his approval. Or rather, I never went anywhere without... without having discussed it with him.

– Prosecutor: So, who was to pay for the rent? Where was the money for the rental agreement coming from?

– Emmanuelli: I understood that the OGP was to reimburse the money to the department of Natural Resources.

...

– Prosecutor: ...and in this case of the building at Barbosa 306, was it negotiated? Yes, or no?

– Emmanuelli: Well, I don't know...

– Prosecutor: Yes, or no?

– Emmanuelli: No, it wasn't negotiated.

– Prosecutor: Expropriated?

– Emmanuelli: No, it wasn't expropriated.

(The above are fragments of the Sentence of the Appellate Court LEXTCA20040317-15 Pueblo v. Aponte Hernández.)

These are some of the things the SIP presented as proof to take the accusation to court. Jorge Aponte Hernández argued in the First Circuit Court that there were errors in the allegations and a total absence of proof. His arguments were based on that R.C. 552 did not necessarily obligate the OGP to expropriate; instead, it allowed negotiations and that the DRNA and not the OGP paid the rental payments. Furthermore, he argued that the state never presented appraisals to substantiate the allegation that the purchase price was too high.

In 2004, the First Circuit Court determined there was sufficient proof:

- According to R.C. 552, Mr. Aponte Hernández, as director of the OGP, was the custodian of the funds assigned and responsible for the state's interests.

- R.C. 552 did not authorize the rental of buildings. Even though the DRNA made the rental payments, they took the money out of accounts for which the OGP was responsible.

- The OGP acquired the building at Barbosa 306 without evaluating any possibility of an expropriation instead of paying the amount that they did in the end.

Seems like pretty solid proof, right?

In 2005, the judge Bárbara Sanfiorenzo decided to exonerate Jorge Aponte Hernández peremptorily, dismissing the charges on lack of sufficient evidence. The case never made it to a trial by jury.

CHAPTER II

Rico's Introspection

I think I'm a nice guy. I say what I think, do what I believe needs to be done, and don't care much about what others will say. My conversations are warm, regardless of whether the topic is complicated or simple. There are no absolutes for me. I'm not afraid to say that I'm a little vain. My shirts are French cuffed, and I like them monogrammed. When I wear a jacket, I believe that the rest of the outfit should be equally well put together. I use a *Mont Blanc* to write with... and for pretty much everything else because I love the brand.

Nothing is as vital for me as being a good person. I love that when I'm walking around the courtroom halls, down the street near my office, or coming back from a restaurant, if anyone recognizes me, they greet me with, "Hey, Rico!" with complete confidence that I'll return the greeting. My colleagues, not only those that work with me but also that present cases against me, feel like they can give me a hug or a hearty handshake out of the courtroom.

I try to be a good friend and an even better acquaintance. Because of this, after the case that I'm discussing here, I was surprised by the radical change. People started snubbing me on the street and saying nasty things behind my back. But, as I said before, I'll still greet those people as warmly as ever. Life is too short for grudges and quarrels.

I enjoy expressing my opinions in public. I never turn down a good discussion, even a religious or political one. What's more, I love politics. It's not that I'm "political" per se; what I'm passionate about is the debate about the responsibilities and obligations of public organizations and about what is fair and just. I was able to express myself in a radio show where I could share my ideas with other panelists. While they didn't always share my opinions, they were worthy of my respect because of their intelligence and seriousness about the beliefs they held.

I love being a lawyer. It makes me so proud to be in the privileged position of defending the rights of those who cannot protect them for themselves.

I'm also thankful for having a profession where I can use my knowledge and experience to ensure punishment for the bad guy, a moment of justice for the victim, and compensation for wrongs committed. It's almost like the Lady of Justice is Wonder Woman, and us lawyers are her sidekicks.

It seems like I'm comparing lawyers to superheroes, and the reality is that when you close a particularly good case and justice is served, it feels that way. Nevertheless, when I'm in a courtroom during an interrogation, I think more like a wrestler. I like wrestling because it's, in fact, theater. I understand that the hits and falls are faked and are not as brutal as they appear, but that doesn't detract from the emotion of an outstanding choreography.

It's the same thing in the courtroom, except the bruising is a bit more severe because your opponent doesn't have the opportunity to practice the moves beforehand. In my office, I have a wrestling mask that my only brother gave me as a gift. I have it in front of my desk to inspire me every time I go to court. Since cases are usually seen in the morning, the inspiration usually lasts just about until I go out to get my coffee.

Almost every day, I get up early to run and walk. It's not that I feel like running or walking; it's because I make myself do it. I did distance running for a time. That was when I was still a student, and like most distance runners, I was a twig. Skinny, I mean. Once I started working, I didn't have enough time to train properly, and by the time I took on the Aponte Hernández case, I was going to the gym every day.

Exercise has always been part of my strategy for concentration. As soon as I put on my running shoes in the morning, my mind starts chewing over all the details of the cases back on my desk. During the closing stages of a case, some of my best examinations have come together during my morning mini-marathons.

Getting back to that coffee... The reality is that I never eat breakfast, so on the days that I'm in the courtroom, I go directly to the courthouse's coffee shop to have my first or second cup of the day. There, I always find colleagues and acquaintances to greet and chat with. Sometimes, I can find new angles or ideas about my cases. I'll pause here to try to describe how I feel when I go to court.

Even though it's been several years, and I'm quite familiar with the courthouse and all the courtrooms, I've never lost the sensation of awe and respect that inspired me the first time I walked in. In some corner of my psyche, I keep the romance with the Lady of Justice alive, and the building where she performs her duties is impressive. The only thing that has changed is that I am no longer intimidated. Now, I feel like a boxer entering the ring for a match.

After the coffee, I usually go to my office; or if it's close to lunchtime, I eat somewhere nearby. When I was a panelist on the radio show, I headed off to the station. After the show, I could finally park myself behind my desk and begin to work on my investigations, write, and process cases. Many times, I've been known to stay so late they would shut off the air conditioning in the building. I'd make do with a couple of fans, because if I'm in the middle of something, I won't leave until I have it just right, even if the office becomes a sauna (thanks to living in the tropics).

I tell you all this so that you have an idea of the person behind the soap opera that started to snowball after I accepted the case of Aponte Hernández, not only in my professional life but in my personal one as well: a workaholic with lots of family responsibilities that I took very seriously. I'm formal and strict with myself. They're all qualities that seem very good if you don't look too closely, but they can undermine the soul of a relationship quite easily.

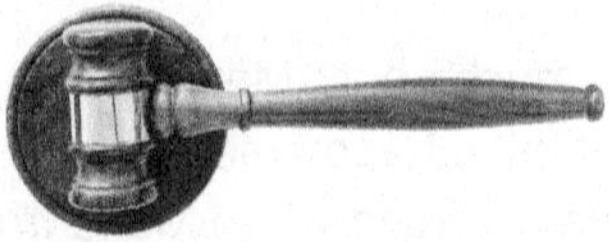

María Irma

Let's go back to the beginning. In 2003, just after I passed the bar exam to become a lawyer, I married whom I thought would be the woman of my life, my friend María Irma. She was an attractive woman with medium-length hair that she always kept straight and a svelte figure. Her eyes were black as night and always had a slightly sad look to them, as if they hid memories that were just as dark. She had a gentle smile, but it never made it to her eyes.

Perhaps it was this mix of tenderness and sadness that awakened my feelings of protection and caring. Once I learned her story, these feelings deepened, adding a sense of pertinence and sincere admiration for how she was able to cope with her past and move forward.

María Irma was raised in a problematic household. Her mother, Medea, wasn't the best role model. Even though she was in the house during her children's formative years, Medea had the bad habit of abandoning María Irma and her brothers for unknown lengths of time. When she was present, she wasn't very maternal.

I don't know much about Medea's first marriage, but María Irma didn't have happy memories from her childhood. Medea divorced when María Irma was still a child. The stories my ex-wife told me had me convinced that Medea didn't deserve the title of "Mother" and described a completely dysfunctional and inappropriate family life.

Eventually, Medea married her second husband, a prominent lawyer called Nero. Once they were established as a couple, they left María Irma and her brothers completely alone. When all this happened, María Irma was just fifteen years old. Her mother never tried to reconnect until her twenty-first birthday.

María Irma, obviously, basically raised herself. In her house, they were always in need–money, food, clothing, school supplies, and above all, supervision. You might think that all the siblings would look after each other, but the reality was much different. It was everyone for themselves, and each one had their plans and agendas.

One of her brothers, of course, took refuge in the underworld, and María Irma had to experience in flesh and blood what it meant to live with someone that used drugs and sold them. Her doorstep was a drug point. Going into her house sometimes meant walking in between those gathered there buying dope, cocaine, heroin, or pills. They weren't exactly upstanding citizens.

Even despite the adverse circumstances, she managed to come out ahead. She graduated from high school and kept on studying, the first person in her generation of the family to make it into university. She wasn't just accepted; she was able to become a Certified Public Account (CPA).

María Irma was studying accounting when we first met and fell in love. It was a fairy tale relationship. We started as friends, then boyfriend and girlfriend. We held hands and stole kisses. We decided that we were meant for each other. It was almost as if destiny had placed us on convergent paths so we would meet. I soon recognized her need to have a sense of security in her life, stability. I also saw her feelings of abandonment. I saw all this while still living within a family environment that was very functional and almost sane in my parents' house.

There came a time that living in her house was martyrdom and a real threat to her safety. Her brother's drug point had become quite popular in front of her house, and there were transactions taking place constantly. Entering and leaving the house could quite easily become a life-or-death situation. Even inside the house, María Irma wasn't safe if one of the "clients" decided to enter.

Things started to heat up on that street. My parents were aware of everything that was happening with my girlfriend, and after a few scares, they offered her safe refuge in our home. María Irma found herself in an oasis of love and support with my family. My parents opened their doors and tried to provide at least a little bit of what she was missing in her life. María Irma saw a stable family environment for the very first time in my house. There, she studied, developed her skills, and blossomed, as did our relationship.

My family

My parents were the opposites of those of María Irma. I had the luck of being raised in a very stable family, in the old ways. There was a lot of discipline but also a lot of love. My parents were very strict, and they taught us values starting from when we were tiny. With faith in God above all, you couldn't get away with anything. That always made me feel very secure about them and their love for me. I learned that I would never go without the necessities, they would always support me in my dreams, and if I ever took a step down the wrong path, they would yank my ear so hard I would need a plastic surgeon.

My parents were a perfect example of life on the straight and narrow. They were both Chilean immigrants and always led their life by what they thought was correct and fair. Both were religious, and their faith in God guided them down the path of the good.

My father came from a long line of equestrians. Together with his father, he learned about raising, training, and caring for the racehorses here in Puerto Rico. Anyone would think that staying in the family business would be the easiest thing for him. On the contrary, he realized just how fragile the industry was before things began to deteriorate, and he decided to become an accountant. He later became a Certified Public Accountant (CPA). Numbers were much more reliable and trustworthy than horses. Looking back on what has happened to the horse racing industry in Puerto Rico, it seems like his decision was more of a premonition.

We don't know that much about my father's family. His father (my grandfather) died of blood cancer (leukemia) at forty-one years old, leaving my father and his siblings behind. Maybe that's why he had such a strong focus on our family life at home. Through hard work and sweat, he grew his client portfolio, later founding his accounting firm.

He never lost his love of animals, but instead of working with them, he was content adopting and sharing his household with the many fortunate dogs that came into our lives. When I began writing this book, he still had his private practice. I can vouch for the long hours he worked because his office was next to mine, and there was a door between our offices that was rarely closed if we were both there.

Unfortunately, my father passed away before the publication of this book. It was a sudden illness, and those are the most painful for those that are left behind. Closing that door between what had been our offices for the last time was one of the most difficult moments of my life.

My mother is 100 percent a lady with all that the title entails. She has an astute mind for business and anything that has to do with jewelry; and she's a great saleswoman. Still, her most significant responsibility has always been being a mother. She never neglected her house or her children. With her firm but loving hand, she took the reins of our education and upbringing, making sure that we grew up to be good people.

Together with my father, she developed a strong family nucleus with endearing ties that have helped us overcome any obstacles. And, following in their steps, we all come together to celebrate when anything extraordinary happens. She's still as beautiful as ever. She walks straight and proud with an enviable figure and a radiant face that shines with external and internal beauty. When my mother smiles, she does so with her whole face, and you can feel her happiness from miles away. She lives feeling proud of her family and us of her. Now that each of her boys has taken their path, she keeps herself entertained with her sales; friends; and, most recently, with her grandchild, my nephew. However, she is still the matriarch of our family.

I was raised in a very structured way. My older brother and I didn't have many opportunities to get into trouble. Although my brother, being the smaller of us, somehow managed to find ways to misbehave. Nevertheless, we were raised with a lot of love, and we didn't fight too much. I don't ever remember resenting my brother in any way, nor did he resent me, as far as I can tell. We have always been more than a family unit. I guess we're more like a clan.

My brother and I are a team. He also studied law and passed the bar but, being a free spirit, he doesn't practice full time. He prefers the business of brunches on the beach and to enjoy the surf and sand of our Caribbean island. Aside from that, his time practicing law happens at a desk he has next to mine. Yes, in the same office that was adjacent to my father's. See what I'm saying about the clan thing?

My mother and father were also a team, but all of us together are an unstoppable force. We were taught to make our way without owing anything to anyone. The expectation was to make a living doing good deeds, helping others, and never taking advantage of circumstances.

I've always tried to live up to these expectations, but I'm no saint. When I decided to study law, there was a great motivation to ensure justice was served. Still, I was also motivated by a drive to litigate, interrogate, and create overwhelmingly convincing dialogue when talking to a witness or the jury.

I love the constant interplay between intellect and emotion, juggling your instincts with the facts you gathered. It was a substantial part of my drive to become a lawyer. This is why I decided to attend civil cases in the Federal Court before a jury. Maybe the confidence my mother instilled in me made me seek out a career where I could fly the flag of justice without keeping quiet about my opinions, where I could tell my opponent off in a very polite and educated way. Certainly in a way that my mother would approve of.

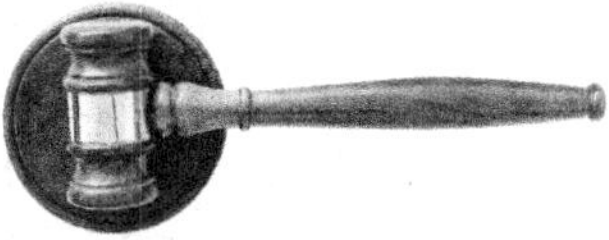

Married

So, getting back to my time as a youngster in love, this upbringing of strict moral standards and values got me thinking that maybe it was my duty to help María Irma be happier. I felt that not only was it fate that put us on the same path but also that it was an opportunity to practice being the great gentlemen that my parents had taught me to be.

My romance with María Irma flowed easily, and we understood each other quite well. When we were alone, and it was just us, everything was peachy. We didn't have any big falling out, and the decision to get married surprised no one. I graduated from the Faculty of Law at the Inter American University of Puerto Rico in July of 2002 and took my bar exam during September that very same year. Without knowing if I had even passed the bar or not, I bought an apartment that very September of 2002, and we were married in January of 2003. Thank God, at the last minute, I received news that I passed the bar on the first try, and I was sworn into the legal profession in January of 2003.

We had our apartment and began our life as a couple. Like I mentioned before, when it was just us, things went pretty well. The problems started when her mother, Medea, came back into her life.

Medea was still a young woman; she looked more like she could be María Irma's sister instead of her mother. She had devoted herself to enjoying her youth and living her own life without worrying about being a mother. It was almost as if she didn't even have children. She placed a lot of importance on her physical appearance during that time, and it showed.

Medea spent some time on the prowl, but she eventually made a life with her husband, Nero. Nevertheless, as soon as María Irma graduated as an accountant and passed her exam to become a CPA, Medea saw an opportunity to take advantage of her daughter's success. Little by little, she began interfering with our lives.

She was always an egotistical woman, which I guess was evident when she abandoned her children to run away and get married, traveling the world without a second thought for her family. I discovered, after our marriage, that Medea was also nosy, meddling, and jealous of her own daughter's happiness. That part was the most shocking for me because after not caring for her daughter's well-being, one would think that seeing her happy would relieve some of her mother's guilt. But no, she never felt guilty at all. She thought that she never did anything wrong and, what's more, she could not leave her daughter in peace.

She began a campaign to slander my reputation as a husband. She started to plant the seeds of discord in María Irma, telling her that I had no ambition. She said this because I wasn't looking for a position that would make us economically privileged.

So, it turned out that Medea's second husband, Nero, wasn't the best person in the world, either. Well, I guess that goes without saying since he whisked his wife away from her children and never allocated any quality time for them. Nero was also a prominent negotiator and a two-faced con artist. He seemed like a likable and happy person when,sin reality, he was just a shark.

Nero associated closely with a friend in a position of power. His friend, Lot, was the mayor of one of the island's important cities, where they grew up together. Lot was one of those people who comes from a long line of powerful political opportunists, quick to take advantage of any situation, and where the strings of power and influence were already woven in his favor. Lot's city was like his own little country, and his word was law. Few dared to cross him until he fell under his weight and lost his power.

Nero never took a public office, but he did become one of Lot's trusted advisors. As part of his duties for the mayor, Nero was able to accumulate quite a lot of money and create positions and nominations. Medea had a plan for me to take one of these positions. She thought that I should work for Nero and, indirectly, for Lot. She assured me that my salary would be attractive enough to offer María Irma the carefree and sheltered life that Medea wanted for her daughter. She didn't care that the position had nothing to do with my career or vocation. Medea was also looking out for herself, wanting to be the in-law of someone in excellent financial standing. It goes without saying that I never accepted the job offer.

After I was sworn in, I began working as a lawyer in a private firm that worked with financial collections cases. I worked there from January to September, and I ran away from that job as soon as I had the chance. It wasn't a bad job, but it was just total boredom. I didn't study all that time to sit behind a desk where the only thing you're striving for is to take people's money.

During that time, the Department of Justice had a shortage of people to work on federal civil cases. I was completely bilingual and available, so I began working in the litigation office of the Department of Justice. I had a full schedule of long hours and not much money to show for it.

María Irma was my faithful companion during my difficult years at university, and she knew very well how involved I would get with things that I was passionate about. I would pour my heart and soul into my work without thinking of details like eating, sleeping, or spending time with my partner. For better or worse (I'm not saying it was the healthiest option), she knew that, as my wife, she had to share me with my work, my parents, and my exercise routine. She also knew that I wasn't motivated by money.

Eventually, she began working for my father to supplement our household income. A year before our separation, she had quit working at my father's office because she had found another job that paid better.

Medea and Nero brought to the surface many pre-existing problems between María Irma and me that we had always ignored. María Irma is a competitive person, and she measures herself based on what other people think of her. She was already tired of losing me whenever there was a challenging or exciting case. She was naturally insecure and was quite fearful of being poor because of the way she grew up. And she was her mother's daughter after all.

On the other hand, I wasn't willing to be manipulated by my in-laws, but I didn't see how that had affected María Irma. I thought she would understand my need to live my life my way. After all, nothing should have come as a surprise. She knew who she married. What I failed to do was reassure her about her insecurities while I was defending my position. I didn't see how the fears and traumas of her childhood interfered with the way she perceived the advice of her mother.

These things started to upset the harmony of our marriage, and the relationship began to lose its shine. It wasn't that we stopped loving each other overnight. Over the years, these tiny droplets of unhappiness began to erode our relationship so slowly that we didn't even notice.

María Irma never did build her self-esteem and confidence to a point where she could take care of her own emotional needs and break away from her codependent tendencies. Since she didn't have the tools to cope with her insecurities, she turned against me.

> I became the cause of her problems and the bearer of her attacks—and with good reason. I never put her first, and I never put myself in her shoes. I felt attacked, pushed, and like I was the only victim in the situation when, in reality, we were both victims and attackers.

I'm explaining all of this so that our eventual separation and divorce doesn't seem like something sudden or unexpected. I also don't think that Jorge Aponte Hernández's case was the cause. It was more like a catalyst.

CHAPTER III

The People vs. Aponte is now Aponte vs. the SIP

Getting back to the lawsuit—after the case of The People vs. Aponte Hernández was thrown out of court by judge Sanfiorenzo, the SIP's panel decided to appeal the decision in the Appellate Court of Puerto Rico, a logical step seeing the amount of evidence that the judge ignored. The other Independent Investigators of the SIP withdrew the appeal before the Appellate Court could make their decision. The governor expressed that, in his opinion, the case should have never gone to court in the first place and implied it involved political persecution.

When someone in a political position of power makes public remarks like these, they are fully aware of the severity of the repercussions. I do not doubt that Governor Acevedo Vilá said what he said hoping to create a movement favoring Aponte Hernández.

He didn't have to wait long for the results of his comments. They provoked the resignation of the president of the SIP's panel, Crisanta González Seda. The office terminated the contracts of prosecutors assigned to the case, and the SIP's office was left practically empty. Jorge Aponte Hernández took advantage of that moment to sue the Office of the Panel of the SIP and the three lawyers involved with the case in the Federal Court for the District of Puerto Rico.

In his claim, submitted in October of 2006, Jorge Aponte Hernández alleged that prosecutors Ana P. Cruz Vélez, Héctor M. Montañez Reyes and José Pérez Rodríguez had worked on his case in a malicious and retaliatory way. The claim included section 1983 (deprivation of rights and privileges), 1985 (conspiracy), and 1986 (negligence to prevent) from Title 42 - Public Health and Welfare from the United States Code. The lawsuit also included the then governor of Puerto Rico, Aníbal Acevedo Vilá.

Aponte Hernández was claiming $33 million in compensation for damages because he was, in his opinion, a victim of a "malicious accusation, fraud, a systemic malicious conspiracy, and of being condemned for a non-existent crime" when he was accused and processed at the state level for buying a building on Barbosa Avenue at a price well above appraisal.

Aponte Hernández alleged that his case should have never gone to court since the prosecutors didn't have sufficient evidence to prove him guilty. The fact that the prosecutors decided to continue with the case despite the lack of evidence, according to Aponte Hernández, constituted a violation of his civil rights.

Court cases are assigned via an electronic lottery, that is to say, at random. At first, this case was assigned to the federal judge Francisco Besosa, who had recently taken the position (he was sworn in on October 2nd, 2006).

Things got off to a bad start right away.

The first thing to be done in cases like this is to present the motion to dismiss. Meaning the defender asks the court to throw out the case entirely due to a lack of evidence to justify the process. A motion to dismiss can be presented at any time during the process. Still, in practice, they tend to happen towards the beginning of the trial because the reason that's most commonly given for the dismissal is that the initial presentation of the plaintiff contains fundamental errors or issues that can invalidate the case.

My team and I came out swinging right from the start. The motion for dismissal that we presented was twenty-seven pages long. In it, we explained, among other things, that the case should be dismissed because the plaintiff failed to make a claim that entitled him to compensation.

The motion for dismissal attacked some of the arguments presented by Aponte Hernández. For example, we defended the legality of the Independent Commission to Investigate Government Transactions, better known as the "Blue Ribbon Committee" created by the then governor Sila María Calderón.

We also highlighted that this entity was validated in 2002 by the First Circuit Court of Appeals in Boston during a case levied by Aponte himself against the members the "Blue Ribbon Committee" entitled Aponte vs. David Noriega-Rodríguez; Ileana Colón-Carlo; Carmen Rita Vélez-Borrás; Pedro Galarza; Pedro López-Oliver; Angel Hermida.

The motion also postulated that Aponte Hernández did not allege any violation of the federal law of civil rights and further pointed out that there was just cause to process Aponte Hernández, as validated in November of 2002 by a judge until the court absolved it in 2005.

Furthermore, the motion claimed that the prosecutors were granted immunity for actions taken in the execution of their duties and that the existence of a conspiracy is impossible since probable cause had already been determined.

The errors or grounds for dismissal, in particular, were related to the doctrine of immunity granted to the independent prosecutors. In general terms, the independent prosecutors had immunity under the civil rights laws in their duty to raise an accusation and for their actions during the trial.

I'm using all the titles and terms correctly because, even though this book might not end up in the hands of a lawyer, I want everyone to understand the validity of the work we had done.

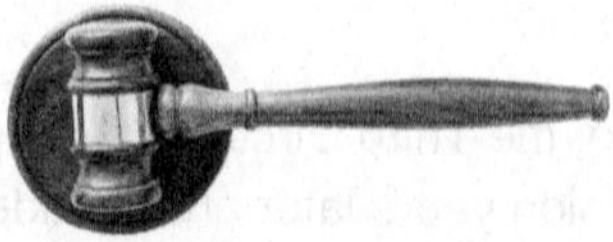

Prosecutor's Immunity

Historically, the law recognizes the need to protect judges and other legal professionals involved in the judicial process from the possibility of lawsuits based on the performance of their legal or quasi-legal duties. This applies to the prosecutors in question.At the beginning of the last century, the Second Circuit of the Appellate Court decided that a federal prosecutor's immunity is absolute based on the principles of public politics. The public interest requires that those who occupy important positions in the judicial branch in a court case and identify with the judicial department of the government can speak and act freely and without fear in the course of executing their official duties. That court determined that those people should not be vulnerable to any private suits, just as judges, witnesses, and jury members are not.

Furthermore, the Third Circuit of the Appellate Court upheld this decision years later and broadened the definition to remove the distinction between a federal prosecutor and a state prosecutor.

Item 7, Article 3 of Law Number 2 of the 23 of February of 1988 as amended, known as the Law of the Panel of the Special Independent Prosecutor, says, "[...] the members of the Panel are to be considered as public servants in respect to their actions in performing their functions, obligations, and prerogatives under the protection of this Law. They will have quasi-judicial immunity in their individual capacity while performing their duties. They will also have immunity equal to that of the members of the executive cabinet."

Nevertheless, during the '90s, the Supreme Court of the United States determined that the prosecutor's immunity is not absolute when it concerns damages like those described in section 1983 of title 42 of the code. This was a completely different case, where the accusation against the prosecutors was for fabricating evidence and giving false testimony during a press conference.

It's a tricky knot to unravel because the court, in that case, concluded that the prosecutor's absolute immunity only applied to their functions as a defender of the state once the trial was in motion but did not apply to their duties as an official investigator or administrator to prepare for the case.

So, the immunity is no longer absolute. It is conditioned on there not being any negligent or malicious actions taken by the prosecutor as part of their official duties, especially during the investigation phase of the trial. It's the same as the immunity offered to a witness, where they supply testimony in exchange for freedom from accusation. That immunity is revoked if the witness is caught lying. Then, not only are they guilty of their original crime but they would also be accused of perjury.

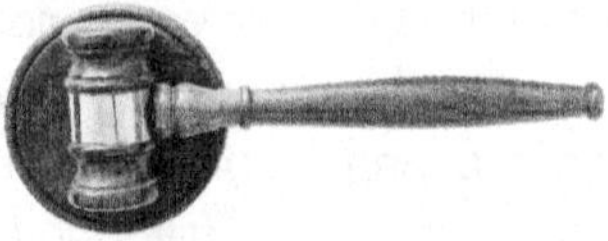

The lawsuit

Suddenly, and without warning, in February of 2007, the case was transferred to the judge José A. Fusté, who was the presiding judge of the Federal Court for the District of Puerto Rico.

I do not doubt that this occurred because Fusté wanted to attend to the case personally.

On April 2nd, 2007, the then president of the senate, Kenneth McClintock, approved for a senator of the New Progressive Party, or PNP, Pedro Rosselló, to recruit Jorge Aponte Hernández as a financial advisor with a contract for thirty hours. Rosselló was the President of the Legislative Conference of the PNP and a key figure during the consideration of the governmental budget. Even though Jorge Aponte's brother was the President of the House of Representatives, this same house made the arrangements to avoid problems with the anti-nepotism law. Just with that, you can see the amount of influence they had then.

In June of 2007, Aponte Hernández requested access to the documents of the OGP, of which not much information is available. In general terms, Aponte requested access to a long list of documents. The then head of the organization, José Guillermo Dávila, denied the request saying that compiling all the documents would have placed an unreasonable burden on the organization and that the request was too broad. Furthermore, we had already filed a motion to dismiss the case, and this additional request for discovery of proof was unnecessary.

Fusté never explained his decision to grant Aponte's request and order Dávila to produce the documents. In his determination, he never specifically mentioned the records that the other side requested.

In July of 2007, the court ordered Jorge Aponte Hernández to retain the services of one or more lawyers to represent him legally during the case.

In September 2007, Judge Fusté made a surprising announcement scheduling the trial for February 2008. That was when John F. Nevarez Esq., brother of Pedro Rosselló's wife, became Aponte's legal representation.

Remember how the US Supreme Court ruled in the '90s that the prosecutor's immunity was not absolute in a specific instance of the code? It was this same ruling that Judge Fusté decided to use in September 2007 to choose not to dismiss the charges against Ana P. Cruz Vélez and Héctor M. Montañez Reyes.

The court decided to uphold the allegations related to the civil rights violations and the suit for damages against the aforementioned ex-prosecutors as individuals. That was when the hard work started, building a defense for a case plagued by injustices and the mistreatment of the accused and myself.

By October of 2007, Aponte presented a motion in which he accused me personally of obstructing the process of discovery of evidence. Us canceling some last-minute dispositions because of my health brought about this little "hissy fit."

Almost immediately, we had to present a motion asking for a gag order against Aponte Hernández's lawyers to curtail their insulting language against the defendants. Among other things, they were making highly pejorative allegations where they even blamed people for being part of a conspiracy even though they had nothing to do with the case. It was war.

In November of 2007, Aponte Hernández's representation requested access to the computers of the Office of the Panel for Special Independent Prosecutors because as part of the discovery of evidence, they had asked for the minutes of the meetings of the SIP between March 2001 and December of 2006. As we never produced these meeting minutes, they requested the computer's hard drives.

Judge Fusté agreed to this request on December 17th, 2007, which was imprudent, in my opinion. It showed how the balance of justice swayed to one side because of the judge. Those computers contained privileged information, and asking for full access could only be an attempt to harm the Office of the SIP. Keep in mind that those computers stored information about all the cases pending for the Panel. It would be interesting to know if today, in 2020, any federal judge would agree to a request like that.

On January 3rd, 2008, I asked Judge Fusté to reconsider his decision, to consider it an error of law because the documents and information requested included confidential and protected information. That information was protected by the immunity clauses of the United States Constitution. The request was obviously a fishing expedition to snoop around on other pending cases in the Office of the Panel. The information requested was entirely irrelevant for the case at hand.

I was able to secure a protection order, which limited Aponte's representation's access to the SIP's computers with an additional clause that assigned Aponte Hernández full responsibility for disclosing privileged information he had access to. As far as I was concerned, this was a strategy to intimidate us, and what I achieved was to put some limits in place.

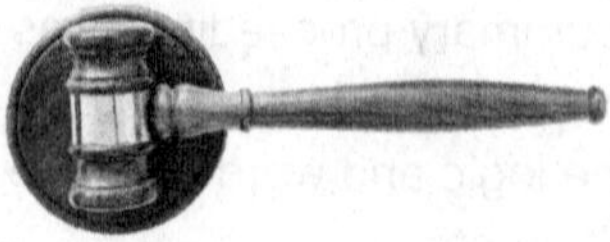

How we came to trial

As part of our defense, our next action was to present a request for a summary proceeding where we asked for the case dismissal again, this time with evidence. We presented the summary proceeding on the basis that the doctrine of immunity protected the prosecutors' actions; that there was no fraudulent or fabricated evidence in the case since Aponte's defense approved the evidence presented in court in the earlier trial; and that the elements of malicious accusation and retaliation by the prosecutors were unsubstantiated and nothing more than allegations by the plaintiff since the prosecutors only did their job, as defined by law without any element of malice or vengeful intent.

Keep in mind that up to this point, even though the case was supposedly going to court in February, there was no trial in sight. We were still getting ready for the fight and definitely not ready to enter the ring. The creation of the summary proceedings was the primary focus of all the motions and investigations that took place up until then. The logic and wording of the document consumed my thoughts.

Now, looking back on that time, it's a miracle that I didn't have any mishaps driving or even walking around near my building in Hato Rey because I was on autopilot autopilot. If anyone greeted me during that time and I didn't answer, I am belatedly asking for forgiveness. Believe me when I say that I never saw you or heard you, and it wasn't intentional.

The District Court denied the summary proceedings on January 28th, 2008. Judge Fusté said there was no immunity for the prosecutors, and he understood that it should be up to a jury to decide if their actions were negligent or not. In his denial of the summary proceedings, it was implicit that he, as a judge, would not take part in the decision-making process. Instead, the decision would be entirely in the hands of the jury.

That same day, we appealed to the First Circuit Court in Boston, but they denied our request as well. On January 30th, 2008, we presented a motion for a continuance to postpone the proceedings. They answered the very next day, January 31st, with another denial. Then, we were left with no other options but to go to trial. But, the trial was scheduled for February 4th. That gave us just three days! We had only the weekend to prepare for it.

So, we put on our gloves and got ready for the fight.

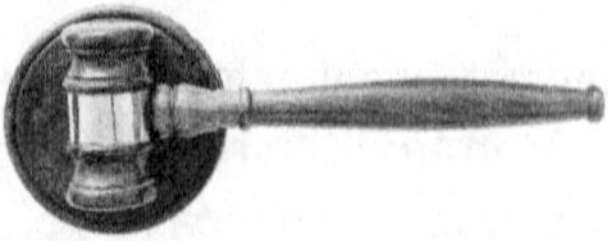

My life during the case

When I took on the case in 2006, I had never even read of a case that had anything to do with suing a prosecutor. I couldn't find any kind of guide on how to carry out this type of case, defending independent prosecutors. I did find some cases that were dismissed and never brought to trial. In the First Circuit, there were no precedents that had a political and partisan context like they had argued in this case. In other words, we had to start from scratch.

As Director of Legal Affairs in the Department of Justice of Puerto Rico, I usually supervised other lawyers assigned to different cases. In this case, it was assigned to me, making me completely responsible for it.

At that time, I didn't have any experienced lawyers under my supervision. They all had passed the bar and were waiting to be sworn in and receive their state or federal licenses.

One of the lawyers waiting for her federal license was Maraliz Vázquez Marrero. She had the luck (perhaps the bad luck) of helping me with my case's process. She was on board from the very first motion for dismissal. It was she who developed the arguments for the immunity of the prosecutors. Ms. Vázquez did much of the legal investigations, the evidence's organization, and structuring of the interrogations. But she still couldn't sign anything, so I was the only one signing and submitting.

The ex-prosecutor Ana P. Cruz Vélez, who was part of the group of defendants in this lawsuit, was always available to help gather evidence, clearly explaining the sequence of events for things that had happened almost five years ago. I never met the other defendant, Héctor M. Montañez Reyes. He was very sick during that time and wasn't able to attend even one of the depositions.

Ms. Vázquez Marrero worked tirelessly and was a crucial part of the entire process. However, it was her very first court case. It was a great way to direct her and prepare her for her future career as a lawyer. Still, it also placed additional responsibilities on my shoulders since I was in the role of guide and mentor while I was preparing my case.

By the end of 2007, I was already in the process of my divorce. I moved back into my parents' house and had limited access to my possessions since they were in the apartment where María Irma was still living. I agreed to the divorce once I finally accepted that there was no way to repair our relationship. I hired two lawyers, recommended by my mother, who were specialists in family law, and detached myself from the process. The only thing I did was read the papers they presented to me.

My parents knew that there would be a rift between María Irma and me before I did. Although they never said anything directly about our relationship and always stayed out of our affairs, they told me more than once, "Think carefully about how things are going because we don't think you're happy. You're not growing with her." Once María Irma succeeded in graduating and launching her career as an accountant, she detached herself from our life together. I didn't want to accept it at first, and it took me a while to realize what was happening, but my parents saw everything.

> Then, just at the climax of the most intense and challenging part of the case, I was in a spare room in my parents' house, living like a nomad, without even a desk, and just trying to ignore the disaster that was my marriage.

In my office, as a supervisor, I still had to direct all the other cases that were pending and in progress. The Aponte Hernández case was one of the seventy or eighty cases under my supervision. The fact that I was working on one of the cases alone had nothing to do with my responsibility to attend to all of them. That meant that my office hours were 9:00 a.m. to 10:00 p.m. if I was lucky, then I was off to a little bar in Miramar, where I would keep working until the wee hours of the morning, beer in hand.

A week before the trial, the process had consumed me to the point that it changed all of my routines. There was no more exercising, I almost didn't sleep, and I practically lived in the office. I lost almost thirty pounds. Eating became optional, and what I did eat was junk. During that time, my life became a whirlwind of work that consumed everything and left no time or space for anything or anyone else. I ate, drank, slept, and breathed that case. I stopped seeing my friends and was constantly distracted whenever I wasn't immersed in my paperwork or behind my computer screen. I became a shadow of myself.

My mother began to worry because she saw that I was becoming agitated, nervous, skinny, and just running from one thing to the next. But my father was my rock. His faith was unshakable. Such was his trust in me that he placed a bet with one of his acquaintances. That person said that the courts would award Aponte Hernández one million dollars. Straight-faced, my father said he should put his money where his mouth was because he was betting that I would win the case. Obviously, I knew nothing of this at the time, and when I found out about it later, I didn't find it funny at all. I don't think my expressions of displeasure affected his mood very much after he had already won the bet money.

In my professional life, I began to understand that the repercussions for attending to the case against Aponte Hernández were significant. There was a real risk of retaliation when, after the elections, the government would be controlled by the other party. At that point in time, we had a divided government. The governor was Aníbal Acevedo Vilá, from the Popular Democratic Party, or PPD in Spanish, but the PNP controlled the Senate and the House of Representatives. José Aponte Hernández was the House's President and the plaintiff's brother, and he even visited the courtroom occasionally during the trial.

It was a very controversial government term, and it was clear that in 2008 the government would fall into the hands of the PNP. There were some contentious movements. I was causing trouble for some people in important places and with influential connections. There were a lot of external ties. You have to remember that Jorge Aponte Hernández directed the OGP, the office that distributed the fiscal budget for the government; had a contract as the advisor for Pedro Rosselló, who was an ex-governor; and his brother was in a position of power in the government.

What convinced me that my career as a public servant was at risk was Aponte's comments during his deposition, his body language, how he branded us as politicians, and how he played his hand. The animosity wasn't limited to him but rather included his whole team. There were also a lot of rumors about his ill intentions that unfortunately turned out to be true.

The Trial

Once the trial began, Aponte Hernández took the stand to testify along with his witnesses that included his ex-assistant, Juan Emmanuelli; the original prosecutor in his first case; the lawyer that had represented him then; the appraiser; and the owner of the property in question, as well as the two ex-prosecutors, Cruz Vélez y Pérez Rodríguez.

As I had explained before, Héctor M. Montañez was quite ill at the time, so the evidence presented for the defense was limited to Ana P. Cruz Vélez' testimony. For everything else, the defense focused on cross-examination of the plaintiff's witnesses. It was a carefully thought-out strategy, as we had put forth the notion that the defense had nothing to prove.

Near the end of the proceedings, and before presenting the case to the jury, Judge Fusté expressed his opinion about the case. The jury wasn't present at the time, but for historical purposes, it's important that you all know how the judge expressed himself. What follows is an unedited excerpt from the trial's official transcript.

***

—Well, let me first say this. I am convinced as to one of the defendants, Mr. Pérez—Mr. Pérez' involvement here was a few days before the trial started. He was an assistant to Montañez. He had no participation in the

investigation of the case, no evidence otherwise, and under those circumstances and under the case law, his–if you want to call it, his quasi-judicial intervention in the context of being a deputy prosecutor gives him absolute immunity.

There is no question about it, and I'm going to dismiss the case against outright, against Mr. Pérez. Mr. Pérez doesn't belong in this case.

We're going to talk about the other part of the case. Let me first say this because–because I am very disillusioned and shocked by the deficiencies, if you will, that I find in the presentation of this case and in the defense of this case. The most important questions in this trial have been asked by me, and not by the lawyers. That's a fact.

And I've done it because I have an obligation to make certain that some sort of basic justice is done in this case, because that's my mission. That's my mission.

And I tell you one thing, I've looked at this case back and forth and I've looked at this evidence, and I am totally convinced as a lawyer, as a Judge, that the prosecution of Mr. Aponte was a total abuse. A total abuse. There was no reason in law or in fact to proceed with that prosecution. No reason in fact and in law.

I am totally convinced, totally convinced that other–other implications and other reasons were behind this prosecution. There is no question about it.

Remember that I was in charge of the Blue Ribbon case to begin with, and I know exactly what went on there. And that case reminded me always of a–not of a jurisdiction under the United States flag, but reminded me of a jurisdiction under a third world country with no Constitutional rights of any kind. And that is a fact. That is a fact.

The prosecutors under the Federal case law can be divided between two different kinds or under placement of two different labels. You have, first, those of Mr. Pérez, the quasi-judicial, the ones who get an investigation from police officers, from detectives, from FBI agents, from DEA agents, and they prosecute.

And, in this case, the other difference is prosecutors who are also investigators, prosecutors who are also doing the work of the police officer. And this is exactly what happened here with at least two, which are Ms. Cruz and Mr. Montañez.

Any lawyer worth his salt or her salt knew or should have known, should have known that there was no reason to proceed with this case. There was nothing on this record, and Judge Bárbara Sanfiorenzo was totally correct.

I read that transcript of the trial, and it's a shame that a case like that went to trial under the U.S. flag. Believe me, it was. And it's up to the jury now to decide as to Montañez and Cruz whether indeed these two prosecutors trampled upon the rights of Mr. Aponte in maliciously, if you will, carelessly, trying to obtain the filing of a criminal case against all odds under these circumstances. And that's exactly what the jury will have to decide in this case.

The Judge is convinced that something is really wrong here, but of course I'm not deciding this case. The jury has to decide this case, and I will instruct the jury accordingly.

Yes, I think this is a case of malicious prosecution. Yes, I think this is a case in which prosecutors overdid it and overdid it for God knows what reasons. And that case should never have been tried, and this case is going to the jury for those reasons. It's as simple as that.

So we're going to bring the jury back–I'll tell you more. Puerto Rico canons of ethics put upon lawyers the burden of never, ever–never, ever inducing a Court to error. And I think that the District Court was induced to error. The Supreme Court was induced to error. The Court of Appeals was induced to error. And the Supreme Court also.

And don't talk to me about procedural postures, because I'm totally convinced that that's exactly what happened in this case. So the motion for judgment of acquittal–for judgment as a matter of law in the case of Mr. Pérez I granted. He can leave. He's finished. But the case against the other two is going to go before the jury.

***

In his tirade, the judge admitted his prejudice against the actions taken by Cruz and Montañez, calling them negligent and malicious. This would have been disastrous if the jury was present at that time. Nevertheless, the judge was very restrained in his expressions when he spoke to the jury to give them their instructions on how to reach the final verdict.

> The jury did not take long in their deliberations. Soon after, they decided in favor of the defendants, dismissing the case. We had won.

Judge Fusté was so angry afterward that he kicked the door to the courtroom open as he left.

After the court delivered the verdict, ex-SIP Ana Paulina Cruz Vélez accused Judge José A. Fusté of being biased in limiting her testimony, prohibiting her from presenting the state rulings against the plaintiff, and preventing instructions from being given to the jury regarding the immunities granted to prosecutors.

"Justice was served, the judge, and I'll say it wherever I can, was very abusive," said Cruz. "I understand that the judge was biased, unfair, didn't give clear instruction about the law, and had his mind made up," she added (Daniel Rivera Vargas, *El Nuevo Día*, February 11th, 2008). Everything that Ana said was true. I was there, and it's all there, in black and white in the court transcript.

Three days after the verdict, my divorce was final.

CHAPTER IV

After the trial—my new reality

In 2008, the government changed hands, exactly as everyone knew it would. The new governor was Luis Fortuño of the PNP. The beginning of his term marked the end of an era for me. Before all the political turmoil and knowing that I touched some problematic and sensitive spots during the case against Aponte Hernandez, I decided to get out of litigation and asked to be transferred to the Assistant Attorney General's office. I chose that office in particular to learn more about the appellate process.

That's when I understood that the retaliation against me had already begun. When I arrived at my new job, I was placed in the tiniest cubicle possible; my desk almost didn't fit in it. They had brought all my files and put them in that tiny space as well. At the end of the day, there was hardly any room for me.

All of my colleagues started distancing themselves from me. I was told before when working the Aponte Hernández case that I was swimming in deep waters. I hadn't understood what they were really telling me: they weren't going to swim in those waters, and I would have to go at it alone. Now that I was in my new position, many of the coworkers that were always on my side pulled a complete 180° and turned their backs on me.

These were moments of deep introspection. I wouldn't be honest if I said that things like this didn't affect me. Yeah, I felt it, and I resented it. After all, as I said in the first place, I'm a good guy. I'm loyal and frank. I would hope for the same from my friends and coworkers. To see how they changed showed me that they had never been sincere.

They were only looking to take advantage of our professional relationship when I was in a position of power. I promoted and gave salary increases to these colleagues, and I helped them reach their aspirations to higher positions. Once I was on the beach, literally, all those little leeches just disappeared. They even avoided me in the hallways! And to think that some of them now have federal jobs because of me. Today, I can say good riddance. But then, I was shaken to see how they ran, both in fear and for political gain.

Then came the bullying. I had three direct supervisors, the attorney, and two assistant attorneys. One of them decided to make my life hell. Who knows why? Honestly, I think the reason behind all the bullying was to make me uncomfortable enough that I would resign.

That person, who will remain nameless, would come into my office wearing very low-cut tops and park her bust on my shoulder. She developed a certain clumsiness around me, and everything would fall to the floor. When she bent down to pick things up, she always made sure she was either facing me and showing me her breasts or turned around in her very tight skirts, making sure that everything was on display.

My coworkers told me that she had gone into my office to rifle through my things while I was out. She asked me intimate questions about my private life. She called me at all hours of the night to talk about things that weren't urgent. She told me that she felt alone, that her husband paid no attention to her, and she asked me if I was with someone. Before leaving the office, she would change into tight exercise clothes and walk by me.

I ended up accusing her of sexual harassment, but you can imagine the discomfort and resentment it caused when I began working in the office again daily.

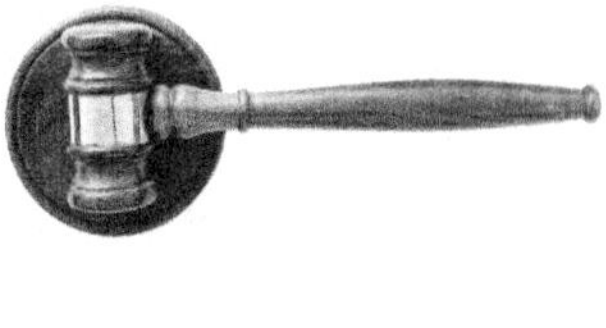

Rico's evolution

I didn't last long in the Attorney General's office. After the sexual harassment case, I got involved in a nasty automobile accident. I won't try to dress it up—it was a difficult situation that I wasn't proud of. But, it was also a staggering moment in my life that led me to make many important decisions and forced me to change direction.

When the accident happened, I became aware of how fragile my situation was publicly and how easy it was for my enemies to create severe problems for me. Until then, I never appeared in the media and was far from being a public figure. However, once I got out from under the mess caused by the accident, I started putting myself in the limelight on purpose. I know it's a strategy that confused many people, but the essential part for me was to regain control of my life. Before someone could put words in my mouth, I would speak for myself and let my opinion be heard.

I started challenging the Puerto Rican establishment and those who would do me harm, expressing my opinions to force their replies. I wanted to see how far they were willing to go. I didn't like being in a vulnerable position.

In 2011, the circus of the campaigns for the new election was underway. And again, there was a wind of change in the powers that be. Finally, after several interviews, I had a federal position assured and was ready to move.

The result of my movements and my public expressions was that my enemies called ICE and immigration, so they would fire me before I could take office. Then, after making sure that I would never get a job in any government agency or public office, they went to the trouble of spreading their "opinion" about me at all the most prominent law firms. The result was that all the doors were slammed shut in my face, not only in the public sector but in the private one as well.

It was a low blow. All of my life, I had thought of myself as a public servant. The motivation for my career up until that point was precisely that–to bring justice for the citizens from inside the government. Take the bull by the horns, as they say.

On the other hand, I had always thought that the way to progress and success was working for someone else. Perhaps it's part of the collective consciousness of living in a colony, the idea that you need to have a boss.

Either way, all of a sudden, I saw myself with no options. I didn't have a job with the federal government or the state government, nor could I find a position in the private legal offices. So, on May 15th, 2011, I began my private practice and became an entrepreneur.

It was the beginning of a great adventure where I learned to survive with a laptop and a plastic table. I started in the very same office I have now, except it didn't have anything in it other than my will to weather the storm. Every time I looked at the empty spaces, the lack of furniture, decoration, and people, I was inspired to go out there and be successful. I didn't need to prove anything to anyone; I was out there for my satisfaction and to achieve my own goals, not only for myself but also for my family that had always supported me.

I began to offer courses in different educational institutions and redoubled my presence in the media. I got into radio thanks to one of my classmates producing a radio show to analyze the elections in 2012. That was Lourdes Torres, and thanks to her invitation, I began to participate in her show, *"1140 millas por hora*" ("1140 miles per hour") on the local station 11Q.

My segments were about international politics, the relationship between Puerto Rico and the United States, federal politics, and things like that. That set me apart because back then, nobody was talking about those subjects on radio or television. The first clients for my private practice started showing up in less than six months. They are excellent and loyal clients that are still with me to this day.

On that radio show, I was able to polish my skills as an analyst and interviewer. I had the opportunity to interview such candidates as San Juan Mayor Carmen Yulín, who had been bitten by a dog during her campaigning the day before, and who nobody thought would ever be elected to be mayor of San Juan. I also interviewed Alejandro García Padilla, Jennifer González, and Ricardo Rosselló, among others.

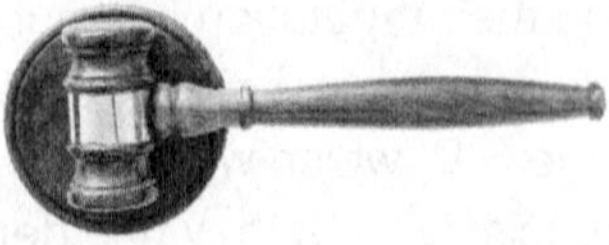

What happened to the SIP?

As you remember, I was a faithful believer in the mission of the Office of the Panel for the Special Independent prosecutor (SIP). That was the primary motivation behind my defense of the prosecutors from the accusations made by Jorge Aponte Hernández. As far as I'm concerned, the Office is of the utmost importance for protecting the victims of crimes perpetrated by government members. I'm also a firm believer in the way the SIP operated at the time of the trial.

However, once Luis Fortuño rose to power, many changes were implemented that affected the integrity of the SIP's services. The office was politicized as soon as they started appointing members directly from the Senate. So, that was the beginning of my disillusionment from what I had considered a model of law and justice.

Those appointments to the Panel led to the perpetuation of the same prosecutors and Panel to the point of tarnishing their reputation and public image. It's absurd and a little ironic that the PNP postulated that the PPD politicized the SIP, which was untrue. But later, the PNP achieved precisely what they had denounced and under their government.

The original objective of the SIP was lost. The office was supposed to be completely independent and neutral. Now, some prosecutors have municipal contracts. What do you think would happen if there was a case against the mayor that gave them the contract? The SIP is creating cases for political reasons entirely without merit and losing them. As a result, their success rate should be abysmal. I say should be because there are no public statistics of their cases.

Now, the public's only reliable resources are the government of the United States and the federal resources available to do the work that the SIP can no longer do. From 2011 until today, corruption cases go one of two ways: either the SIP loses the case, or the federal government resolves it. The SIP has only been able to process a few sexual harassment cases against government members, like mayors, but the evidence was practically forced.

But, I'm not the kind of person to point out problems without offering solutions. I think there is a new way to save the SIP. I believe the current office should be closed. New legislation needs to be developed with particular ethical rules that apply to a new Special Independent Prosecutors Oversight Board. The prosecutors cannot be government employees. They could even be elected by nomination, but never by political affiliation.

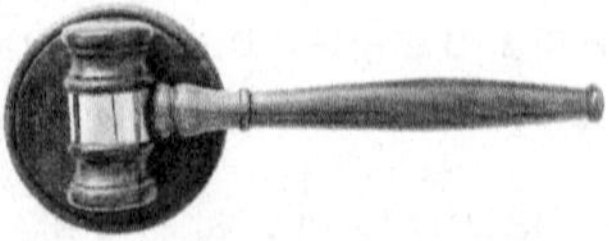

Who is Rico today?

At the end of the day, I am who I am because I threw myself into the thick of the fray and decided to defend the SIP from the government. I learned more than I lost. If I had to make a list of all the changes, the good and the bad, there would be more good things on that list.

On the one hand, I resolved a marriage that had turned into something toxic and was more harmful than beneficial. The last time I saw María Irma was around 2011, and it didn't make a big impression on me. I just struck out on my path and left everything else behind.

On the other hand, I learned to better evaluate my relationships with my coworkers, friends, and relatives and understand that the motivations behind kind gestures or words of admiration are not always the same motivations I might have. I'm honest; not everyone else is. I can live with that.

I understood that success doesn't depend on your boss, but rather on oneself. So, I stopped being colonized in my career goals and started being an independent republic with a story full of successes.

I recognized that my family is, and always will be, a group of people that I can count on at any time, the same way they can count on me. We are a clan.

I can accept that I'm not infallible and that I'm not always in control of everything.

On the other hand, I discovered how to take control over situations in my life once I start feeling vulnerable.

In the end, I lost some sleep and some of the people in my life, but I gained experience, astuteness, resilience, and respect.

Was it worth it?

Totally.

AUTHOR'S PROFILE

Attorney Valenzuela-Alvarado was admitted to the legal profession in January 2003, first working at private practice and thereafter in Puerto Rico's Department of Justice (2003-2011). During his first months as an admitted Attorney, (January 2003 - September 2003) Mr. Valenzuela-Alvarado worked as an Associate Attorney in O'NEILL & GILMORE, P.S.C. (FORMER OFG&P-O). He was in charge of the Sears, CitiCapital (A Citi Group Division), and One Stop Prescriptions, Inc. accounts, working with cases such as collections, labor and employment, torts, contracts, appellate practice, and request of permissions at the P.R. Department of Health for pharmacies. He also assisted in Federal litigation, specifically in torts, and obtained litigation experience.

Thereafter, while working in civil litigation at the Department of Justice (2003), Attorney Valenzuela-Alvarado was appointed by the then secretary of justice as Director of Legal Affairs (2006-2009) in charge of civil state and federal litigation of around twelve to twenty-four attorneys and supporting personnel. Attorney Valenzuela-Alvarado managed cases before the Federal District Court for the District of Puerto Rico (jury trials, and injunctions), the Federal Bankruptcy Court for the District of Puerto Rico (adversary proceedings), the State Courts, and supervised cases filed at other jurisdictions. After January 2009, Attorney Valenzuela-Alvarado served in an interim basis as Director of Legal Affairs.

Then, Attorney Valenzuela-Alvarado was appointed Assistant Solicitor General (2009-2011), handling appeals before the Puerto Rico Appeals Court, the Supreme Court, and the First Circuit Court of Appeals. He also handled and conducted ethics complaints against attorneys before the Puerto Rico Supreme Court in writing and in litigation, before appointed commissioners.

In May 2011, Attorney José Enrico Valenzuela-Alvarado founded Valenzuela-Alvarado, LLC. Among his duties in private practice, attorney Valenzuela-Alvarado has worked representing plaintiffs and defendants in the federal (diversity and federal question cases) and state courts, including appellate practice, and as Official Examiner in labor and employment cases at the local Department of Education.

In addition, Attorney Valenzuela-Alvarado has worked since 2011 *pro bono* as District Justice before the Board of Directors of Phi Alpha Delta Law Fraternity International, specifically in District XXVII-Puerto Rico, representing the three law schools in Puerto Rico: University of Puerto Rico School of Law, Inter American University of Puerto Rico School of Law, and Pontifical University of Puerto Rico School of Law.

Attorney Valenzuela-Alvarado also created and currently is providing the following Continuing Legal Education Seminars, all approved by the Puerto Rico Supreme Court:

- "The Summary Judgment at the Federal Forum, the best intent to dismiss a case," (P.R. Supreme Court No. LITI-2007-210)
- "Federal Civil Rights Act in Puerto Rico, General Pre-Trial Theory and Practice," (P.R. Supreme Court No. LITI-2010-419)

- *"Aspectos Prácticos en Quejas y Querellas Éticas ante el Tribunal Supremo de P.R.,"* (P.R. Supreme Court No. ETI-2007-49)
- *"ABA Model Rules of Professional Conduct y los Cánones de ética Profesional en el Siglo XXI,"* (P.R. Supreme Court No. ETI-2014-420)
- "El Dilema de los Honrarios de Abogados," (P.R. Supreme Court No. ETI-2012-271)
- *"La Litigación en los Medios ante los Cánones de ética Profesional,"* (P.R. Supreme Court No. ETI-2012-260)
- *"Conflictos de Intereses, ética y Civilidad en la Litigación,"* (P.R. Supreme Court No. ETI-2012-206)
- "*Jurisdicción Federal*: The Basics," (P.R. Supreme Court No. LITI-2011-447)
- *"Efectos del Informe del Departamento de Justicia Federal ante la Litigación de Derechos Civiles en Puerto Rico,"* (P.R. Supreme Court No. CONST-2008-29)

Also, Attorney Valenzuela-Alvarado has the following publications:

- "Federal Jurisdiction v. Abstention, Who Prevails?," XLIII NÚM. 2 REV. JUR. U.I.P.R. 279 INTER-AMERICAN UNIVERSITY OF PUERTO RICO SCHOOL OF LAW (September 2009)
- "Federal Civil Rights in Puerto Rico, General Pre-Trial Theory And Praxis In The New Century," XLIV NÚM. 2 REV. JUR. U.I.P.R. 197 INTER-

AMERICAN UNIVERSITY OF PUERTO RICO SCHOOL OF LAW (September 2010)

- "How To Defend a Prosecutor at The Federal Forum in A Civil Rights Complaint?," LEY Y FORO, COLEGIO DE ABOGADOS DE PUERTO RICO (August 2008)
- *"El Contrato de Transacción en los Pleitos de Clase,"* XXXVII NÚM. I REV. JUR. U.I.P.R. 165 (2002)
- *"El término prescriptivo y su retroactividad ante las quejas y querellas éticas contra abogados en Puerto Rico,"* (9 octubre 2016), https://aldia.microjuris.com/2016/10/09/el-termino-prescriptivo-y-su-retroactividad-ante-las-quejas-y-querellas-eticas-contra-abogados-en-puerto-rico/
- *"La asignación de abogados de oficio en casos penales vs. la representación efectiva de acusados en Puerto Rico,"* (5 noviembre 2016), https://aldia.microjuris.com/2016/11/05/la-asignacion-de-abogados-de-oficio-en-casos-penales-vs-la-representacion-efectiva-de-acusados-en-puerto-rico/

Finally, Attorney Valenzuela-Alvarado also participated *pro bono* in the television show *Sistema TV Informa* (news program) at Sistema Universitario Ana G. Méndez, and in *Wapa.TV* (Noticentro.TV) at Channel 4. He collaborated with *Mi Gente* (talk show) at Canal 13-Tele Oro, as legal and political analyst once a week. He collaborates on *Nación Z, Noticentro al Amanecer* by WAPA TV, and on productions by WAPA América. Telemundo de Puerto Rico and Telemundo Orlando trust in his legal perspectives and call on him frequently to share them with their audiences. All his content is shared via social media, where he continues the discussion.

José Enrico Valenzuela-Alvarado was born in San Juan, Puerto Rico. His deep Chilean roots come from his father, José Alamiro Valenzuela-Fuentes (RIP 1951-2019), and his mother, Patricia Alvarado-Fernández, whose inscrutable values built a strong family environment where he grew up with this brother, Christian Valenzuela-Alvarado, Esq. His constant desire to inform and serve drives him to share daily with the media, where he contextualizes daily events carefully and ethically. There, he shows that by sharing knowledge, we all grow together.

Made in United States
North Haven, CT
04 November 2026

21732950R00059